# What's in this book

This book belongs to

T0351516

_____

# 现在几点？ What's the time?

## 学习内容 Contents

### 沟通 Communication

询问时间
Ask about the time

表示时间
Tell the time

背景介绍：
由于地球上不同地区白天与黑夜出现的时间不同，于是有了时区的划分。图为身处不同时区的人们在做不同的事。

## 生词 New words

| ★ | 早上 | early morning |
| ★ | 上午 | morning |
| ★ | 下午 | afternoon |
| ★ | 晚上 | evening, night |
| ★ | 现在 | now |
| ★ | 两 | two |
| ★ | 点 | o'clock |
| ★ | 半 | half |
| ★ | 分 | minute |
| | 中午 | noon |
| | 号 | date |

## 句式 Sentence patterns

现在几点？
What's the time?

现在早上八点半。
It is 8:30 in the morning.

## 跨学科学习 Project

了解时区的概念，计算时差
Learn about time zones and calculate time differences

## 文化 Cultures

古代中国时辰
The hours in ancient China.

## Get ready

**1** What time does your school start?

**2** How often do you check the time in a day?

**3** Do you know what 'time zone' means?

故事大意：
本课介绍了时区与时间。
地球被划分为 24 个时区，
每个时区的标准时间不
同，故每个时区内的人们
做着不同的事。

-11　-10　-9　-8　-7　-6　-5　-4　-3　-2

xiàn zài jǐ diǎn
现在几点？

1:00　2:00　3:00　4:00　5:00　6:00　7:00　8:00　9:00　10:0

参考问题和答案：

1　What is Big Ben asking the boy? (What time it is now.)

2　What time is shown on Big Ben? (12 o'clock.)

-1  0  +1  +2  +3  +4  +5  +6  +7  +8  +9  +10  +11  +12

xiàn zài shí èr diǎn
现在十二点。

参考问题和答案：

1  How does the boy answer Big Ben? (It is 12 o'clock now.)

2  How many time zones can you see on the world map? (There are 24 time zones on the map.)

3  Which time zone is Big Ben in? How do you know? (It is in the standard time zone because the clock above the 0 time zone also shows 12 o'clock.)

:00  12:00  13:00  14:00  15:00  16:00  9.00  20:00  21:00  22:00  23:00  24:00

北京（中国）
UTC/GMT +8

日出以后，大概6:00
至9:00或10:00间的
时间我们叫"早上"。

**zǎo shang bā diǎn bàn**
# 早上八点半。

当一个小时刚好过了一半时，我们说
"X点半"，也可以说"X点三十分"。

洛杉矶（美国）
UTC/GMT -8

HOLLYWOOD

**xià wǔ sì diǎn bàn**
# 下午四点半。

"下午"即中午到日落之间的时间，
大概从 12:00 到 18:00。

**shàng wǔ shí diǎn bàn**
# 上午十点半。

早上之后，正午之前，即9:00或
10:00到12:00之间的时间我们叫
"上午"。

布里斯班（澳大利亚）
UTC/GMT +10

参考问题和答案：
1 What is Big Ben asking the children?
(What time it is now.)
2 Do the children have the same answers?
(No, they have different answers.)

**ziàn zài jǐ diǎn**
# 现在几点？

布宜诺斯艾利斯（阿根廷）
UTC/GMT -3

**wǎn shang jiǔ diǎn bàn**
# 晚上九点半。

"晚上"指日落后到第二天日出前的时间，
大概从 18:00 到第二天 06:00。

zǎo shang liù diǎn shí wǔ fēn

# 早上六点十五分。

"分"即分钟，一分钟
等于 60 秒。描述时间
时，我们一般说"X 点
Y 分"，Y 从一到六十。

wǎn shang qī diǎn sì shí wǔ fēn

# 晚上七点四十五分。

shàng wǔ jiǔ diǎn shí wǔ fēn

# 上午九点十五分。

wǎn shang shí diǎn shí wǔ fēn

# 晚上十点十五分。

参考问题和答案：

1  Find the boy who is sleeping. What is the time there? (It is fifteen minutes past ten in the evening./It is ten fifteen in the evening.)

2  Are the children doing the same thing? Why? (No, they are not. Because they are in different time zones. )

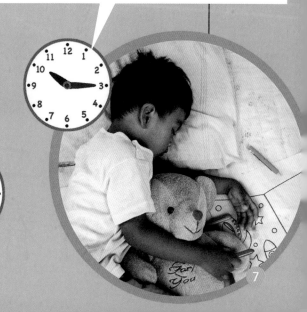

xià wǔ liǎng diǎn shí wǔ fēn

# 下午两点十五分。

"两"即数目"二"，用在"点"之前时，
我们说"两点"，不说"二点"。

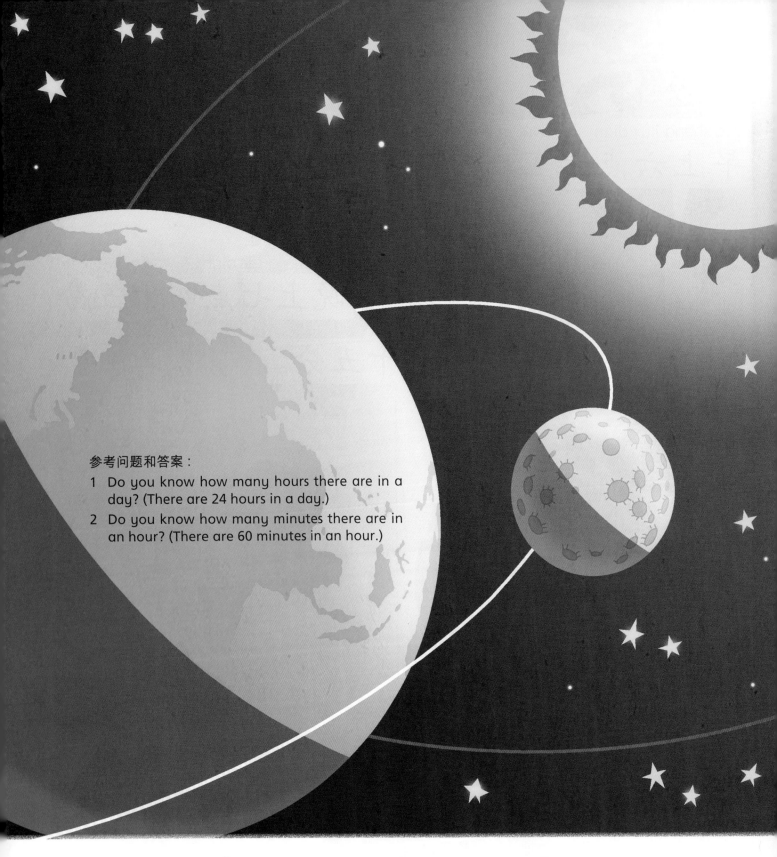

参考问题和答案：

1 Do you know how many hours there are in a day? (There are 24 hours in a day.)

2 Do you know how many minutes there are in an hour? (There are 60 minutes in an hour.)

一天有二十四小时。
一小时有六十分钟。

参考问题和答案：

1 What is the time now in your time zone? (It is half past nine in the morning./It is eight o'clock in the evening.)

2 Where are you? (I am at school in Hong Kong./I am at home in the United States.)

3 What are you doing now? (I am having a Chinese class./I am reading with my mother.)

现在几点？你在哪里？
你在做什么？

# Let's think

**1** ## Look at the time and match the clocks.

可以让学生一边连线，一边用中文说出时钟上的时间。

参考句式："早上/上午/下午/晚上……点……分。"

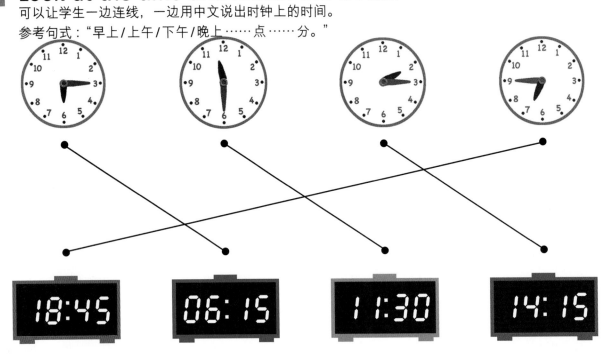

**2** ## Tell your friend which type of clock you like and why. Design your clock on the right.

Analogue clock

Digital clock

参考答案：
I like analogue clocks because I like the hands on the clock. /I like digital clocks better because the numbers give me the exact time.

# New words

说日期时，我们可以说"日"，也可以说"号"，如"一月十五号"。

12:00左右（11:00至13:00）的时间我们一般叫"中午"。

中午

十五 一月

号

**1** Learn the new words.

早上

点

上午

半

下午

分

两

晚上

现在

**2** Look at the time and write the letters. You may use the letters more than once. 提醒学生注意区分图片中的白天和黑夜。"X点三十分"也可以说"X点半"。

a 半　　b 点　　c 分　　d 现在　　e 晚上　　f 上午

__d__ 是 __f__ 九 __b__ 三十 __c__（九点 __a__）。

__d__ 是 __e__ 九 __b__ 五十五 __c__。

# 听听说说 Listen and say

🎧 03 **1** Listen and mark the time on the clocks.

🎧 04 **2** Look at the pictures. Listen to the stor

第一题录音稿：
1 现在是十二点。
2 现在是下午两点半。
3 男孩：现在是不是下午五点二十分？
  女孩：不是，现在是下午五点四十分。
4 男孩：现在几点？
  女孩：早上八点四十五分。

1

2

3

4

nd say.

第二题参考问题和答案：

1  Why does Hao Hao confirm Dad's return date? (He knows there is a time difference between the two places.)

2  Do you know anyone from another time zone? What is the time difference between you and him/her? (Yes, my grandparents live in China. The time difference between us is thirteen hours.)

## 3  Match the sentences to the pictures. Say to your friend.

a  他们下午四点半看书。

b  她们上午十一点画画。

c  他们下午三点十五分踢足球。

在学生完成配对练习后，让学生遮住上方中文，看图片说出完整的句子。

# Task

Talk about your daily routines and activities with your friend.
Complete the table.    鼓励学生用汉字来填写全部空格。

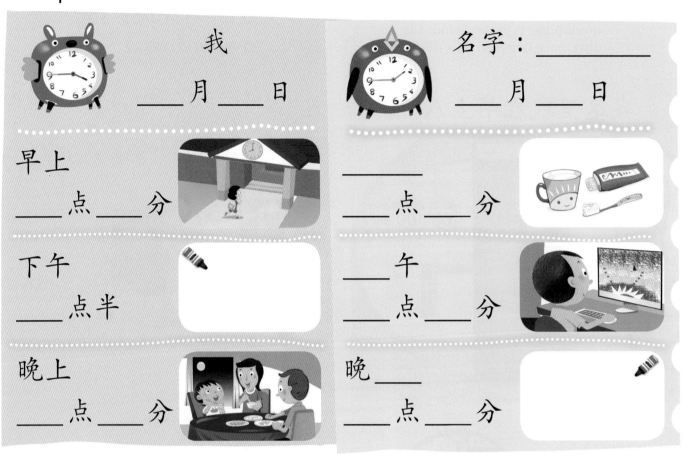

# Game

## Listen to your friend and act out the time.

游戏方法：

老师在纸盘上写数字，贴到墙上形成钟面。学生站在中间，根据老师的指令，把手臂当做时针来表示时间。

9:30

7:45

12:00

3:30

2:15

8:15

2:00

10:45

# Song

🎧 Listen and sing.

现在几点？

现在一点、两点、三点、四点。

现在几点？

现在五点半、六点半、七点半、八点半。

现在几点？

现在九点、十点、十一点、十二点。

## 课堂用语 Classroom language

两人一组。

Two people form a group.

四人一组。

Four people form a group.

# 写一写 Write

**1** Review and trace the strokes. 提醒学生先回忆笔画名称及其写法，再进行描写。

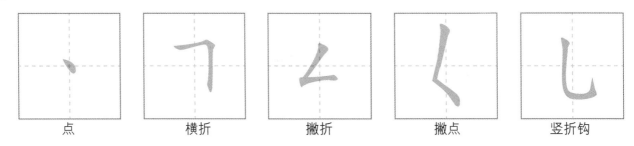

| 点 | 横折 | 撇折 | 撇点 | 竖折钩 |

**2** Learn the component. Trace ⺗ to complete the characters.

"四点底"表示地面上熊熊燃烧的火焰或是动物的尾巴。老师应提醒学生注意第一点与其他三个点的方向不一样。

灬　点　燕　熊　糕

**3** Write the time in Chinese and the missing dots. How many dots are missing? There are nine dots missing.

七 点　　十 点　　两点

五点　　八 点　　十二 点

**4** Trace and write the character.

丶 卜 占 占 占 占
点 点 点

点

| 点 | 点 | 点 |
|---|---|---|
| | | |

The same character can have more than one meaning.

Discuss the meanings of the characters in **red** with your friend. 同一字词的不同含义要根据具体语境来判断。

你在**哪里**?
Indicate location.

三**点**

表示时间，多指小时。

十**分**

表示时间，指分钟。

你在**做**什么?
Indicate an activity/ action you are doing

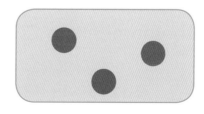

三**点**

多指小而圆的物体或痕迹。

十**分**

即"分数"，用数字来表示等级高低。

多元学习 Connections

## Cultures

**1** Learn about the hours in ancient China. Colour the first two-hour period red and the last one blue.

"十二地支"（见下）与"天干"（甲、乙、丙、丁、戊、己、庚、辛、壬、癸）相搭配，表示年、月、日的次序，也用来表示时间。

古代中国，两个小时称为一个"时辰"，一天共十二个"时辰"。

In ancient China, the 24-hour day was divided into 12 two-hour periods. It started at 11 o'clock at night.

红色

蓝色

日晷

Ancient Chinese clock

古代，人们根据太阳光下晷针投射在刻度盘上的阴影来判断时间。

**2** How many of your classmates were born at each of the two-hour period? Write the numbers in Chinese.

| 23-1 | 1-3 | 3-5 | 5-7 | 7-9 | 9-11 | 11-13 | 13-15 | 15-17 | 17-19 | 19-21 | 21-23 |
|---|---|---|---|---|---|---|---|---|---|---|---|
| 子 | 丑 | 寅 | 卯 | 辰 | 巳 | 午 | 未 | 申 | 酉 | 戌 | 亥 |
|  |  |  |  |  |  |  |  |  |  |  |  |

# Project

全球共24个时区，以英国格林尼治天文台所在的0度经线（即本初子午线）为中心，东西延伸7.5度，即每15度划分为一个时区。为了避开地区分界线，时区的形状呈不规则。同一时区内，不同地区的时间相同；不同时区间的时间，小时不同，分钟相同。

## What's the time? Write below and report.

PRIME MERIDIAN

The Earth is divided into 24 time zones starting from the prime meridian.

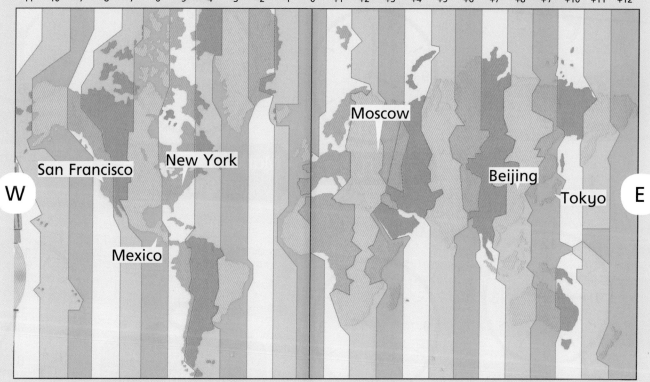

Going one zone west we have to take away 1 hour.

Going one zone east we have to add 1 hour.

## When it's 1p.m. in London, what's the time in:

先让学生完成练习，再用完整的中文句子说出每个地方的时间。

参考句式："……（现在）是早上/上午/中午/下午/晚上……"

- New York?          8 a.m.
- San Francisco?      5 a.m.
- Tokyo?              10 p.m.
- Beijing?            9 p.m.

- Moscow?            3 p.m.
- Mexico?            6 a.m.

Can you say the times in Chinese?

温习 Checkpoint

游戏方法：
老师提醒学生根据虚线方向来一次完成题目。题型要求有：用
完整的中文回答问题、根据要求补充时针、写汉字。

**1** Help Hao Hao answer the questions in Chinese and complete the tasks.

现在几点？
现在上午八点。

Mark '上午九点半' on the clock.

现在几点？
现在上午十点半/三十分。

现在几点？
现在下午两点四十五分。

现在几点？
现在下午两点半/三十分。

Say 'afternoon' in Chinese.
下午

现在几点？
现在中午十二点二十五分。

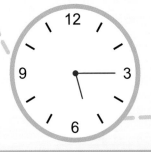

Mark '下午五点十五分' on the clock.

Say 'evening' in Chinese.
晚上

现在几点？
现在晚上九点四十五分。

三 点

Write '3:00' in Chinese.

20

评核方法：
学生两人一组，互相考察评价表内单词和句子的听说读写。交际沟通部分由老师朗读要求，学生再互相对话。如果达到了某项技能要求，则用色笔将星星或小辣椒涂色。

## 2 Work with your friend. Colour the stars and the chilies.

| Words and sentences | 说 | 读 | 写 |
|---|---|---|---|
| 早上 | ☆ | ☆ | ☆ |
| 上午 | ☆ | ☆ | 🌶 |
| 下午 | ☆ | ☆ | 🌶 |
| 晚上 | ☆ | ☆ | 🌶 |
| 现在 | ☆ | ☆ | 🌶 |
| 两 | ☆ | ☆ | 🌶 |
| 点 | ☆ | ☆ | ☆ |
| 半 | ☆ | ☆ | 🌶 |
| 分 | ☆ | ☆ | 🌶 |
| 中午 | ☆ | 🌶 | 🌶 |
| 天 | ☆ | ☆ | 🌶 |
| 现在几点？ | ☆ | ☆ | 🌶 |
| 现在早上八点半。 | ☆ | ☆ | 🌶 |

| | |
|---|---|
| Ask about the time | ☆ |
| Tell the time | ☆ |

现在几点？

现在上午十一点十五分。

Mark '中午十二点' on the clock.

Write 'What's the time?' in Chinese.

几 点

## 3 What does your teacher say?

评核建议：
根据学生课堂表现，分别给予"太棒了！(Excellent!)"、"不错！(Good!)"或"继续努力！(Work harder!)"的评价，再让学生圈出右边对应的表情，以记录自己的学习情况。

# 分享 Sharing

延伸活动：
1 学生用手遮盖英文，读中文单词，并思考单词意思；
2 学生用手遮盖中文单词，看着英文说出对应的中文单词；
3 学生两人一组，尽量运用下方的中文单词分角色复述故事。

## Words I remember

| 早上 | zǎo shang | early morning |
| 上午 | shàng wǔ | morning |
| 下午 | xià wǔ | afternoon |
| 晚上 | wǎn shang | evening, night |
| 现在 | xiàn zài | now |
| 两 | liǎng | two |
| 点 | diǎn | o'clock |
| 半 | bàn | half |
| 分 | fēn | minute |
| 中午 | zhōng wǔ | noon |
| 号 | hào | date |

## Other words

| | | |
|---|---|---|
| 小时 | xiǎo shí | hour |
| 分钟 | fēn zhōng | minute (as in duration) |
| 在 | zài | (to indicate an action in progress) |
| 做 | zuò | to do |

# OXFORD
## UNIVERSITY PRESS

Oxford University Press is a department of the University of Oxford.
It furthers the University's objective of excellence in research, scholarship,
and education by publishing worldwide. Oxford is a registered trade mark of
Oxford University Press in the UK and in certain other countries

Published in Hong Kong by
Oxford University Press (China) Limited
39th Floor, One Kowloon, 1 Wang Yuen Street, Kowloon Bay,
Hong Kong

Illustrated by Anne Lee, Doris Lee, KK Ng, KY Chan and Wildman

Photographs for reproduction permitted by Dreamstime.com

China National Publications Import & Export (Group) Corporation is an authorized distributor of
Oxford Elementary Chinese.

Please contact content@cnpiec.com.cn or 86-10-65856782

ISBN: 978-0-19-942983-7

10 9 8 7 6 5 4 3 2


Teacher's Edition
ISBN: 978-0-19-082205-7

10 9 8 7 6 5 4 3 2